Contents

First published 2004 by
Walker Books Limited, 87 Vauxhall
Walk, London SE11 5HJ 10 9 8 7 6 5 4 3 2 1
Text © 2004 Jeanne Willis Illustrations © 2004
Lydia Monks The right of Jeanne Willis and Lydia
Monks to be identified as author and illustrator
respectively of this work has been asserted by them in
accordance with the Copyright, Designs and Patents Act
1988 This book has been typeset in Clichee and Tree
Printed in China All rights reserved British Library
Cataloguing in Publication Data: a catalogue record for
this book is available from the British Library
ISBN 0-7445-8682-8

WALKER BOOKS
AND SUBSIDIARIES
LONDON • BOSTON • SYDNEY • AUCKLAND

www.walkerbooks.co.uk

Part One

Bits

"Am I just
a teenage
dirt bag?"
All the nitty-gritty on
growing up and private parts

Q Eek! My body is changing – am I morphing into an alien?

It seems unlikely, but just to make sure, check your symptoms against this chart.

AM I MORPHING INTO AN ALIEN?

1A Have you grown six heads? ☐
1B Is your face getting longer and less babyish? ☐

2A Is your skin green and oozing slime? ☐
2B Is your skin slightly shiny/spotty? ☐

3A Are you covered in thick, green fur? ☐
3B Are you growing little hairs under your arms/down your pants? ☐

4A Are you 50 light-years old? ☐
4B Are you between 8 and 17 years old? ☐

5A Have you recently destroyed another galaxy in a fit of rage? ☐
5B Do you sometimes feel a bit moody and misunderstood? ☐

6A Have you grown a tentacle overnight? ☐
6B Are you growing bumps on your chest? ☐

If you ticked mostly As –
You are turning into an alien. Go back to your planet and take your spaceship with you!

If you ticked mostly Bs –
YAY! You're turning into a woman. Welcome to the wonderful world of puberty!

Q Ooer! I couldn't tick any As or Bs – what's puberty?
Puberty is when your body stops being like a child's and you start to become an adult. The time when it happens is called adolescence. Don't worry if you haven't noticed any changes yet – lots of girls reach puberty when they're about 11, but it can happen any time between 8 and 17.

5

Q Help! How can I tell if I've started puberty?

Some of the changes take place inside you, but others are more obvious. Don't panic – you won't grow a pair of big blancmanges overnight. The changes happen over several years so you've got ages to get used to the gorgeous new grown-up you. Here are some signs to look out for:

growth!

deep voice

1 YOU START GROWING REALLY FAST. Up to 11 cm in one year! Yep, great excuse for buying new clothes!

2 YOUR HIPS GROW WIDER. To make room for a baby one day/to make your bum look cute.

wide hips

3 YOUR VOICE GETS DEEPER. So you can shout at your parents/whisper sweet nothings in someone's ear.

4 YOUR FACE CHANGES SHAPE. So you look old enough to see an 18 film/have more room to put make-up on!

5 YOUR MUSCLES GET STRONGER. So you can carry your shopping.

face shape

6 YOUR BREASTS START TO DEVELOP. To feed babies/fill your bikini.

breasts

hair

7 YOU GROW HAIR IN FUNNY PLACES. God's little joke – no good reason except to increase sales of razors/wax.

8 YOUR PERIODS START. So you can make babies/have an excuse to be moody once a month.

periods

9 YOUR FEELINGS AND EMOTIONS CHANGE. So you can fall in love/fight for your rights/feel like a woman.

Q Help! I'm the shortest girl in my class. I'm sick of being called Titch, and the last time I went to the cinema they wouldn't let me in because I didn't look old enough.

HEY, Shorty!

It can be tough being short – it sometimes feels like everyone's looking down on you. People often assume short people are younger than they are – great when you're 40 but a pain in the butt when you're trying to get into a film that's not a cartoon about fairies.

But listen, it can be just as tough being tall. Everyone expects you to act older than you really are, and trousers are always too short in the leg. At least you can snip the bottoms off yours. Also, don't forget, you haven't finished growing yet if you're under 18. In the meantime, remember there are lots of good things about being a little person. Oh, and next time you go to the flicks, carry some ID to prove you're a big girl really.

GET THIS!
The average British woman is 1.62 m (5 foot 4 inches) tall.

10 GOOD THINGS ABOUT BEING TALL

1 You can reach the top shelf without a ladder.

2 You can get into X-rated movies. (Not that you'd ever do such a thing.)

3 You look great in long skirts.

4 You can look down on people.

5 Everyone wants you in the netball team.

6 Most of the boys in your class have to look up to you.

7 You can borrow your mum's clothes. (She must have some cool ones somewhere.)

8 You are brilliant at the high jump.

9 People think twice about picking on you.

10 You don't have to wear high heels.

GET THIS!

The tallest woman in history was Zeng Jinlian (born 1964, in central China). She was 2.48 m (just over 8 foot).

10

10 GOOD THINGS ABOUT BEING SMALL

1 You have less far to fall.

2 You can get away with a kid's fare on the bus. (Not that you'd ever do such a thing.)

3 Small trainers are cheaper than big ones in the same style.

4 You're never too tall for the guy you fancy.

5 Short people often make great leaders.

6 Your hair doesn't get caught in the springs if you sleep in the bottom bunk.

7 You save pounds on material if you make your own gear.

8 Boys like rescuing you.

9 There's always room for a little one.

10 You have a fantastic excuse for wearing high heels.

The shortest was Pauline Musters ("Princess Pauline", born 1876, in Holland). She was only 61 cm (24 inches) high.

11

Q Every time I throw a moody, my mum says it's my hormones – what's she cackling on about?

Hormones are chemicals in your body that tell it to behave in a certain way. At puberty, sex hormones kick-start all the physical changes that happen to you. They can also affect your emotions. Sometimes they take a while to settle down and you get mood swings. One minute, you're a ray of sunshine, the next, you want to strangle your own mother. Some mothers deserve to be strangled, of course, but mostly they don't mean to wind you up. When your hormones are mucking about, everybody seems out to get you – even the hamster.

Next time you feel like you're going to explode/cry/kill, remember that the food at The Correction Home for Moody Cows really sucks, put that axe down, and try these mood-calming tricks instead:

MOOD-CALMING TRICKS FOR MAD MOMENTS

✳ Beat the fluff out of your pillow.
✳ Dance like a lunatic/go for a run/walk the dog.

* Phone a friend and ask her to talk you down off the ceiling.
* Have a good howl.
* Pamper yourself.
* Put all your feelings down on paper, then tear it into tiny shreds.
* Count to 10.
* Cuddle someone you love.

13

Q I got a detention for calling someone a twat at school – why? I thought it just meant the same as twit.

Oops – what a difference one letter makes! Twat is a slang word for ladies' rude bits, and it's not a very pretty one either. There are loads of them. Some are quite sweet. Others are very rude. Some are simply disgusting! For your eyes only, here is a list...

WARNING!!! Some people find these words very offensive, so don't use them in polite company.

fanny   honeypot

beaver

box   PSSST!   vadge
          What's yours
          called?

tail

twat

pad

14

Q Um, er, so what's the PROPER name for my front bottom?

Most of us have pet names for our privates (see below), but there comes a time when a girl needs to know what's what. Basically, external sex organs (the ones you can see) are called genitals. The proper name for female genitals is the vulva. The best way to see what yours looks like is to examine it gently with clean fingers using a hand mirror.

(Don't try this in Topshop! Find a place with good lighting where you know you won't be disturbed.)

jelly roll

poontang   hole

muff
        pussy

slit   mivvy

        quim
cunt   bush
        minge

snatch   flap

    shrubbery   coochie

crack

WHAT'S WHAT
(diagram of female external sex organs)

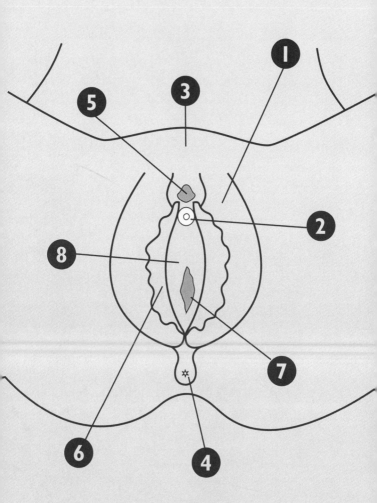

1. OUTER LABIA: Two thick folds of skin with pubic hair growing on them – these protect the inside of your vulva.

2. URINARY OPENING: The opening to the tube leading from your bladder (urethra).

3. MONS: A pad of fat that protects your pubic bone.

4. ANUS: Hole at the end of the digestive tract, where solid waste (poo) comes out.

5. CLITORIS: Very sensitive to touch. It becomes erect – the female equivalent of a penis.

6. INNER LABIA: Thin, hairless inner lips. They are rarely the same size and sometimes stick out. They make lubricating fluid in their glands, which is why they feel moist.

7. VAGINAL OPENING: Tube leading to your internal reproductive organs. It's where the blood comes out when you have a period, where a man puts his penis when you have sex, and where babies come out when they are born. (It may look small but it's very streeeeeeetchy!)

8. HYMEN: Thin layer of skin that partially covers the vaginal opening. An unbroken hymen used to be seen as a sign of virginity, but it isn't – hymens often break during puberty, especially if you play lots of sport.

Q This is a bit of a hairy one: my sister has curly pubes but mine are dead straight and wispy – how weird is that?

Not at all, actually. Pubic hair usually starts off soft and downy. As you get older, it often grows coarse and curly, but there is a fantastic variety of "Downstairs Hairdos". Sometimes it grows a completely different shade from the hair on your head. (This is Mother Nature's way of stopping folk checking your pubes to see if you're a natural blonde.)

GET THIS!
The average vagina is 10 cm (4 inches) long.

1 2 3 4 5 6 7 8 9 10

A Girl's Guide to Downstairs Hairdos

1. THE SMOOTHY: pre-pubescent

2. THE MUFTY TUFTY: scanty blond pubic hair; new growth

3. THE BUBBLE CUT: medium blond curls

4. THE BURNING BUSH: long, fine bushy red hair

5. THE MEXICAN WAVE: thick, black curls

6. THE CURLY-WURLY: profuse, sprawling brown hair

7. SHORT BACK AND SIDES: short, brown, neat triangle

8. THE MOHICAN: grows in neat strip down middle

Q Help! I smell funny down there – is there something wrong with me?

Depends what you mean by funny. A vagina smells kind of musky and salty, even if it's just been washed. Sometimes your natural odour is stronger on certain days, depending on the time of the month. It's caused by sweat, oil glands and cheeky little substances called pheromones, which are carried in your vaginal fluid and are highly attractive to the opposite sex. If you notice a nasty smell (often with an unusual discharge) you may have an infection. If you think you might have, see a doctor. She'll have seen it all before and will be able to treat it easily.

GET THIS!
The French use less soap than any other country in Europe.

20

Q How am I supposed to wash right up inside my vagina?

You aren't! Vaginas are like posh ovens – they clean themselves! They produce special lubricating fluid that does the job perfectly. There's no need to go poking about. All you need to do is bath or shower daily, washing gently between your legs with mild soap – don't use fancy smellies on your delicate bits as it can cause irritation.

If you need to freshen up and you can't get to a shower, give yourself a quick going-over with a soapy flannel or paper towel (rinse carefully and pat dry) or keep some baby wipes in your bag. You can buy special wipes for your feminine area but it's best to avoid the ones with deodorant and perfume.

HOW TO CARE FOR YOUR MUFF

- [ ] HAND WASH ONLY
- [ ] DO NOT USE STRONG DETERGENT
- [ ] DO NOT DRIP-DRY
- [ ] DO NOT RUB HARD
- [ ] PAT DRY WITH CLEAN TOWEL
- [ ] DO NOT DRY-CLEAN
- [ ] DO NOT IRON
- [ ] DO NOT KEEP IN NASTY NYLON KNICKS
- [ ] KEEP IN COTTON UNDIES AND CHANGE DAILY

Q Help! I've got armpits like King Kong. Should I shave?

Some people find armpit hair very attractive, but if you don't like it, that's your business. Get rid! There are several ways of removing hair from your face and body, but before you reach for the razor/lawnmower/hedge-clippers, check out the advantages and disadvantages of each method.

GET THIS!
Humans are related to apes and used to have hair all over their bodies.

Hair-removal techniques

What	How
DRY SHAVING Best for armpits, legs.	Buy an electric razor for women. Plug in, switch on and shave your woolly bits.
WET SHAVING Best for armpits, legs.	Get an easy-grip razor or use a disposable one. Lather skin with mild soap and warm water. Shave downwards for pits, upwards for legs.
SALON WAXING Best for everywhere.	Make an appointment, take your trousers off and lie on the bed in old pants.
HOME COLD WAXING Best for everywhere.	Use strips of ready-waxed Cellophane that you press onto your skin and pull off.
HOME HOT WAXING Best for everywhere.	Wax is usually heated in a microwave or a pan of hot water. You spread warm wax onto your skin, press cotton strips onto the wax and whisk the hairs off.
TWEEZING Best for eyebrows, odd stray hairs.	Buy good quality tweezers. Gently stretch skin, grab hair between tweezers and pull quickly in direction of growth.
HAIR-REMOVING CREAM Best for pits, legs, bikini line.	Always do a patch test first. Smooth cream onto hair, following direction of growth. Leave on for the suggested time, then rinse off.

Pros	Cons
Quick, easy and you can't cut yourself.	Some girls reckon electric razors don't leave skin as smooth.
Quick, cheap, painless and easy to do yourself.	Hair grows back prickly within a few days. It's easy to nick yourself.
Hair doesn't grow back for six weeks. A beautician can reach those awkward places. No mess to clear up.	Pricey. Also, hairs have to be long enough for the wax to grip them.
Cheaper than hot wax, quite effective and you can't burn yourself.	Can be painful and messy. Doesn't work on coarse hair.
Good results if done properly. Hair doesn't grow back for four to six weeks and it grows back soft.	Can be messy, painful and awkward. Risk of scalding with hot wax.
Quick, cheap and effective.	Can be slightly painful and the hair will grow back within days.
Cheap, painless and can give good results. Effects last longer than shaving.	Messy and poo-eeh! Who cut the egg sandwiches?

Q Why does my body have to change? I don't want to grow up!

The reason your body changes is so that one day you can have babies. OK, maybe you'd rather poke pins in your eyes than think about that right now, but hang on a mo – the other thing about growing up is that your mind changes too. And guess what? You'll find yourself wanting to do all the squelchy stuff that used to make you go Yeeeuch! (Honestly, you will!)

True, growing up isn't always a breeze. Most girls (and boys) feel confused and upset at times, but it can also be the best fun you've ever had – if Peter Pan knew what he was missing he'd grow up like a shot!

Remember, you don't have to stop being you just because your body is changing. You can still do everything you love and more!

GET THIS!

The longest beard grown by a lady belonged to Janice Deveree (born 1862). It was 36 cm (14 inches) long.

GOOD THINGS
ABOUT GROWING UP

✪ You can climb trees, jump in puddles and wear high heels. (Not all at the same time though!)

✪ You hold Mum's hand because you love her – not because you're crossing a road.

✪ You're never too old for a goodnight cuddle, but you can stay up late.

✪ You fall in love with a real person instead of a poster.

✪ You get to travel a whole lot further than the postbox.

✪ You get to make your own decisions – even if they suck.

✪ You can be who you want – it's your life!

Part Two

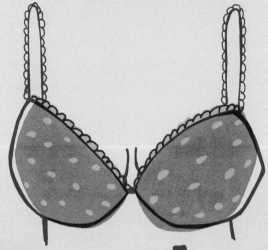

Boobs

"What are these lumpy things on my chest?"

How to be
bosom buddies
with your breasts

Q My brother says my boobs are just made of fat? Is that true?

No, that's what his head is made of. There's a lot more to breasts than meets the eye – show him the diagram below if he doesn't believe you.

MAMMARIES ARE MADE OF THIS

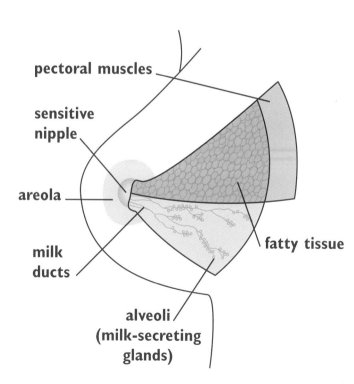

pectoral muscles

sensitive nipple

areola

milk ducts

fatty tissue

alveoli (milk-secreting glands)

ILLUSTRATION OF BREAST DEVELOPMENT

a) First, the nipple and the areola get larger and sometimes darker. (They might ache a bit.)

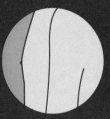

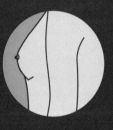

b) Milk ducts and fat tissue form a small, disc-like mound under each nipple and areola. This makes them stick out. (Don't be surprised if one forms before the other – it often happens.)

c) Fat deposits begin to fill out the area and your breasts may start to look pointy. (Maybe a good time to check out the bra counter.)

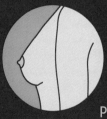

d) Breasts continue to fill out. Sometimes the nipples and areolas form a separate mound and get more pronounced. (Not always, though.)

e) You've got the full set!

Q Help! I'm flat-chested, but my nipples are tender and swollen. Why?

Don't worry! This often happens when your breasts start to develop. Your nipples grow first and they can feel a bit sore at the beginning, but it'll soon pass, promise! In the meantime, try not to knock them when you play netball and fold your arms in the dinner queue to protect them. If they're really killing you, ask your mum for some paracetamol.

Q Mum said she used to have really big boobs till she had me – is she making it up?

What? You don't believe your own mother?! Of course, she could be boasting, in which case the only way to tell for sure is to find a photo of her in a bikini in the olden days. Be warned though, she's probably telling the truth. Bosoms have a habit of changing shape and size during adulthood. Going on the pill, having a baby, or pigging out on cakes can all affect breast size and shape. Sometimes they get smaller; sometimes they get bigger. Some girls even go up a whole cup size just before their period.

Q Help! One of my boobs is bigger than the other. Am I a freak?

No, no, you are not turning into the Hunchfront of Notre Dame. One breast often grows faster than the other, but the other one soon catches up. Having said that, nobody – but nobody – has a truly matching pair, except Barbie (unless they're cheating).

I feel a right **tit!**

There once was a girl from Devizes
Whose BOOBIES were
different sizes.
The one on the right
She would keep out of sight,
But the other won
several prizes.

Q I'm a tomboy. Bosoms don't suit me. What use are they?

You're not the first to ask this question. Amazon women used to cut off their right boobs just so they could fire their arrows straight. True, breasts can get in the way when you're trying to fire an arrow – the upside is that bras make great catapults.

Seriously, Mother Nature didn't give you two bumps on the front for nothing – their main purpose is to make milk. Without it, humans would have died out long ago. OK, you can buy formula milk today, but breastfeeding is thought to be much better for the baby. Breasts also heighten your sexual pleasure, and boys think they're beautiful – even really intelligent boys – and anything that helps you catch your ideal mate has to be good.

Q Help! In winter my nipples stick out and show through my clothes.

Nipples are even better than seaweed at predicting a cold snap, hence the phrase "It's a bit nippy!" They are one of the most sensitive parts of a woman's body.

If it's cold or they are touched, tiny muscles make them go hard (erect). There's nothing you can do to stop it happening. But if you feel embarrassed, avoid tight-fitting tops, cover up with a jacket or wear a T-shirt/vest under your blouse. If it happens during swimming lessons, covering up with a cardy is a no-no. Just take a deep breath and jump in quick! Chances are, no one will notice, and anyway, everyone else's will be sticking out like hat pegs too!

Q My friend says our breasts will fill up with milk when we reach puberty – is it true?

No! You can't make any milk unless you have a baby. The milk-making glands (alveoli) in your breasts don't start working until you become pregnant.

Q I'm 14 and my breasts are really titchy. Will they grow any bigger?

Probably. Breasts don't usually reach their full size until you're about 17. Having said

GET THIS!
Boys' breasts sometimes swell slightly at puberty – but this soon disappears when their hormones settle down.
AH, BLESS!

OOOH, John, what a lovely pair!

that, some of us are never going to be well endowed. If you want your breasts to look bigger, there's no need to stuff a pair of socks down your vest. The right bra can work wonders!

BRA STYLES

Bra with gel inserts

Underwired bra

Push-up bra

Bra with adjustable cleavage

GET THIS

In 1943, actress Jane Russell wore a famous uplift metallic bra in The Outlaw. The film was kept off screen for 6 years for reasons of morality!

Large breasts can weigh over a pound!

Q Help! My boobs are massive. I can't see my feet!

Some girls dream of having big breasts (boys dream about them constantly), but it's no fun if you feel uncomfortable with your body. Even so, don't try and hide your breasts by hunching your shoulders and staring at the floor. It will just give you lousy posture and you'll bash into lampposts.

The best thing to do is buy a bra with really good support. If you can't find what you want in the shops, try catalogues or the

Internet. There are lots of gorgeous bras especially made for bigger-busted girls who don't want to look like their granny – you can even buy styles that "minimize" your bust. Once you've found your perfect bra, put your shoulders back, look the world in the eye and be confident!

There was a young lady called Marge
Whose boobs were as BIG as a barge.
Her twin sister, Jeannie,
Had bosoms so weeny
The boys called them Little and LARGE!

GET THIS!
The term brassière first appeared in American Vogue in 1907.

Q I'm 15, I'm flat-chested and I'm fed up.

Remember that you haven't finished growing yet. The way you feel about your body is bound to change as you grow older. Having small breasts may feel like the end of the world right now, but true happiness doesn't lie in a whopping great pair of bosoms. Ask anyone who's got them. It may make boys notice you more, but wouldn't you rather they noticed your massive personality? If you still feel worried about it in a few years' time, discuss it with your doctor.

You could try wearing breast-enhancers. These are gel-filled moulds that you wear inside your bra to boost you up a few cup sizes. They look a bit like chicken fillets, but under clothes they look and feel like the real thing.

Q I'm sure my boobs are a funny shape. What should they look like?

There are no rules! Breasts come in all different shapes and sizes – just as well, 'cos some folk fancy fried eggs while others go wild for watermelons. Breasts vary more

in appearance than any other part of a woman's body. Even nipples come in a variety of fashionable shades from Barely Black to Princess Pink.

Q Help! I swear I'm a 34B but my bra keeps riding up at the back while my boobs are squishing out of the cups.

According to recent surveys, one in three women wears the wrong-sized bra. To avoid making the same boob, you need to measure yourself properly. See page 42 to find out how.

HOW TO FIND YOUR BRA SIZE

When you buy a bra, you need to know your chest measurement and cup size.

TO FIND YOUR CHEST SIZE

Measure just under your breasts around your rib cage and add 12 cm (5 inches).

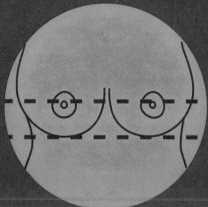

Example: *68 cm (27 inches) + 12 cm (5 inches) = 80 cm (32 inches)*

TO FIND YOUR CUP SIZE

Measure around the fullest part of your breasts. If this is the same as your chest size, you need an A cup. If there is a 2.5 cm (1 inch) difference, you need a B cup. If there is a 5 cm (2 inch) difference, you need a C cup.

Q Help! I've just noticed weird purple lines on my boobs. What are they?

Stretch marks. When your body grows fast, your skin has to stretch to keep up. Sometimes it hasn't got quite enough elastic and you get these purplish lines. They can happen all over the place – most of us have got some somewhere. There's not a lot you can do to prevent them, but they usually fade over time.

Q Help! I'm 14 and my nipples go in instead of out!

Don't worry – if you've got innies they'll probably grow into outies as you develop. Try drawing them out very gently between your finger and thumb every day until they get the general idea, or you can buy a gadget at the chemist's to do this. However, if your nipples suddenly invert when you're fully developed (from 18), go and see a doctor.

43

GOOD THINGS ABOUT BIG BOOBS

* There's no mistaking you for a man.

* They keep your feet dry.

* You get to play the sexy roles in the school play.

* Boys love big ones.

* Small-bosomed girls are jealous of your curves.

* You've always got somewhere to shove your purse.

* You've got something to put in your bikini top.

GOOD THINGS ABOUT SMALL BOOBS

✳ The best things come in small packages.

✳ It saves on suntan lotion, if you go topless.

✳ You get to play Aladdin in the school panto.

✳ You can go on a trampoline without getting black eyes.

✳ Boys love little ones.

✳ Big-bosomed friends are jealous because you don't wobble.

✳ You look fantastic in sports gear.

THE BOOB GALLERY

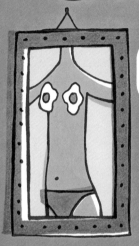

fabulous fried Eggs

Magnificent Melons

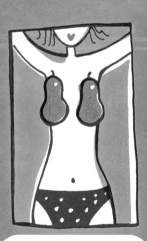

Pouting Peaches

Perfect Pears

Q My boobs aren't very big – do I have to wear a bra?

It's entirely up to you. Some people say that if you don't wear an Over-Shoulder Boulder-Holder it'll ruin your figure. Don't listen to them. The elastic fibres in breasts are gonna stretch and droop with age, even if you sling them up under your chin in a bra from the age of 10.

Having said that, if you have stonking great bazookas, the weight of them may cause the fibres to stretch prematurely, so it's a good idea to rein them in.

Many girls feel more comfortable wearing a bra, especially if they play a lot of sport – it's the ball that's supposed to bounce, not the boobs!

Others like to wear a bra because they prefer the shape it gives them – and they're soooo pretty.

Q I walked past a building site and a workman yelled, "Nice jugs!" at me. Why did he say that?

Basically, he was admiring your breasts, but for some reason, his mum never told him it was bad manners to shout it out loud. If it happens again, just ignore it and walk straight past. There are loads of slang words for breasts, some nicer than others. Just so as you know, here are some of the most common ones...

GET THIS!

Henry VIII's wife, Anne Boleyn, had several breasts. This condition is called polymastia.

Boob Slang

BAPS

KNOCKERS

TITS

BOSOMS

JUGS

BAZOOKAS

PUPPIES

DUGS

UDDERS

BRISTOLS (cockney rhyming slang: Bristol Cities = Titties)

THREEPENNIES (cockney rhyming slang: Threepenny Bits = Tits)

JUBBLIES

ZEPPELINS

PAPS

Part Three

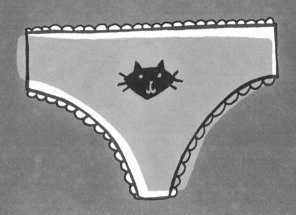

Blobs

"Oh no!
Those were
my best knickers!"

PERIODS:
What, why, and how to cope
without going bright red

Q The girls at school keep talking about periods. What exactly is a period?

Having a period (menstruating) means that every month you lose a small amount of blood through your vagina for a few days. See pages 54 and 55 for a biology lesson!

Bleeding heck!

Q Why do girls have periods and not boys? It isn't fair!

Like it or not, girls are made differently. We can dress like boys, behave like boys, we can even call ourselves Kevin and join the

Hey, Kevin, lend us a tampon!

fire brigade – but there's no escaping the fact that women's bodies are designed to give birth. We don't have to have babies if we don't want to, but isn't it nice to have the choice?

Having periods might seem like a pain in the bum, but it's all part and parcel of being able to start your own family one day.

Q Help! I'm 15 and I haven't started my periods yet. Is there something wrong with me?

Na. Periods can start at any time between the ages of 8 and 17. It usually happens about a year after your breasts develop, but there are no advantages to starting early. If your mum started late, you might too. Also, short, stocky girls tend to come on earlier than tall, thin ones.

WHY IT HAPPENS: Girls are born with hundreds and thousands of eggs stored in their ovaries. You have two ovaries – one on each side of your uterus (see diagrams). When you reach puberty, sex hormones make the eggs ripen. Every month, an egg is released and takes a one-way ticket to your uterus via the uterine tube. Meanwhile, the uterus lining grows thick and cosy, ready for the egg to arrive. If the egg isn't fertilized (i.e. if you don't get pregnant) the egg and the lining disintegrate and pass out through your vagina with some blood. Voilà: you have a period!

When the bleeding stops, the whole thing starts all over again. This is called your menstrual cycle. (As you can see, this has nothing to do with mountain bikes.)

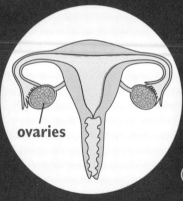

ovaries

1. OVARIES: At puberty, hormones make the eggs (ova) in your ovaries ripen. Once a month, an egg is released (ovulation).

GET THIS!

A single ovum is the size of a full stop.

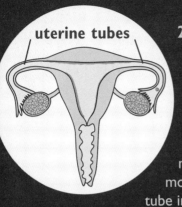

uterine tubes

2. UTERINE (OR FALLOPIAN) TUBES:

If the tasselly end of the nearest tube detects an egg, it draws it inside. Tiny muscles and hairs move the egg down the tube into the uterus.

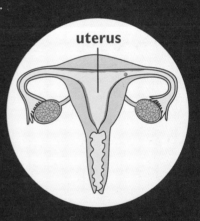

uterus

3. UTERUS (WOMB):

Every month, the uterus lining thickens, ready for a fertilized egg to arrive and grow into a baby.

4. CERVIX & VAGINA (BIRTH CANAL):

If you don't get pregnant, the uterus lining and egg disintegrate and pass out through the cervix and vagina with some blood (menstrual flow). The cervix has a narrow canal (2 mm) running through it which lets sperm in and menstrual fluid out. It stretches enormously when you give birth.

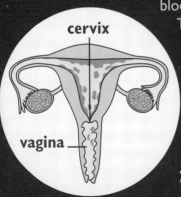

cervix

vagina

Q There was some browny-red stuff in my pants when I went to the loo. What could it be?

The chances are, your period is starting. Period blood is often brown instead of red at first.

Q When you have a period, how long do you bleed for and how much blood do you lose?

Most girls bleed for between 3 and 8 days. The average time is 4 days. The flow of blood is usually heaviest at the beginning and lighter towards the end. You usually lose about 2 tablespoons of blood.

Q I haven't started my periods, but sometimes I get a damp patch which dries whitey-yellow in my knickers – what is it?

Around puberty, glands in your vagina start to produce slippery stuff. This helps to keep it clean and lubricated. Some days, you'll hardly notice it, other times it can get quite damp down below. As long as the discharge isn't smelly and you're not sore or itchy, it's nothing to worry about. It's natural, normal and comes out easily in the wash. However, if you'd rather it didn't gum up your gussets or you're worried it'll show during gym, wear a panty liner.

GET THIS!
48% of women bleed for 3–4 days. 35% bleed for 5–6 days. The rest bleed for 7 days or more.

Q Help! I've just started my periods but I don't know whether to use towels or tampons – what's the difference?

Sanitary towels are soft, absorbent pads that you wear inside your pants. They soak up blood as it leaves your body.

Tampons are absorbent plugs (about 6 cm long) that you put inside your vagina. They catch blood before it leaves your body.

Lots of girls use towels when they first start because they're easy to use, but you can use tampons straight away if you like. Or you can mix and match. Some girls prefer to wear tampons in the day and a towel at night – it's up to you. You can often get free samples from magazines – try out different brands to find the one that's best for you.

Q I can't get my tampon in – what am I doing wrong?

Like most things, it takes practice. Next time you have a period, try the tips on pages 62–63.

Q I love swimming and I'd like to use tampons, but won't they fall out?

Nice muscles!

No way – once a tampon is in place, it won't come out until you pull it out by the string. The muscles in your vagina hold it in place.

SANITARY TOWELS
OR
TAMPONS?

SANITARY TOWELS

✳ They come in different sizes and thicknesses — choose one to suit your shape/the heaviness of your period.

✳ Press-on towels have a sticky strip on the back. Remove the backing paper and press onto the inside of your pants.

✳ Change your towel every few hours, even if your flow is light. Blood is perfectly clean, but once it gets outside your body, bacteria can make it smell.

✳ Don't flush towels down the loo, in case it blocks — bag 'em and bin 'em.

PROs: Easy to use. Effective and comfortable if you choose the right size.

CONs: They can crease or come unstuck. You can't go swimming. Smelly if you don't change them often enough.

TAMPONS

✳ There are two types: one has an applicator, which guides the tampon into your vagina; the other doesn't – you use your finger.

✳ Tampons come in different sizes, from mini to super-plus. The bigger the tampon, the more absorbent it is. Choose the right size for your blood flow.

✳ Once a tampon is inside you, it expands to fit your vagina and prevent any leaks.

✳ A tampon may leak if it needs changing, in which case you may feel a slight bubbling sensation and the removal cord will be blood-stained.

✳ Change your tampon at least every 4–6 hours (first thing in the morning if you wear one at night). Leaving them in too long can cause infection – in rare cases it can cause Toxic Shock Syndrome, a serious illness.

✳ To remove a tampon, you pull it out gently by the cord. You can flush tampons down the loo or bag 'em and bin 'em.

PROs: You can't feel them and they don't show through your clothes. You can go swimming. There's no smell and they're easy to carry because they're so small.

CONs: Some girls have difficulty inserting them. Risk of Toxic Shock Syndrome.

TIPS FOR PUTTING YOUR FIRST TAMPON IN

1 Use the smallest tampon you can find (mini-tampons or lites).

2 Wait until your period is heaviest – the tampon slides in easier.

3 Lubricate the rounded end of the tampon (or tampon applicator) with Vaseline or KY jelly and choose one of the following positions...

The Lone Ranger

Straddle the loo with knees slightly bent and hips pushed forward.

Knees up, Mother Brown

Put one foot up on the toilet seat. If that's too low, try the edge of the bath.

The frog

Squat down on the floor over a hand mirror.

Ribbit! Ribbit! Comfortable? Now you need to do a bit of origami.

4 Use your fingers to unfold all the flaps of skin – there's a vagina in there somewhere, it's just a bit shy.

5 Found it? Yay! Now, hold the rounded tip of the tampon (or applicator) at the entrance with one hand. Remember to aim it towards the bottom of your back. Vaginas are built on a backward slope – you can't put a tampon in as if you were sticking a pencil up your nostril.

6 OK, after 3, you're going to gently push the tampon in as far as it will go with the middle finger of your free hand. Ready?

1...2...3...PUSH!

Is it in? If it's in the right position, you won't be able to feel it. If you can, you just haven't pushed it in far enough.

7 If it still won't go in, no worries! Try again next month. Your hymen may still be unbroken, or maybe all you need to do is relax – if you're tense, your muscles will tighten up, making it harder to put the tampon in.

Q I'm sure people can see my sanitary towel when I wear tight clothes. It's so embarrassing – is there anything I can do?

Try using a different brand – some press-on towels are almost as thin as panty liners these days, yet they can be just as absorbent as thicker towels.

If your flow is very heavy, try using tampons – they are invisible under the tightest clothes because you wear them internally.

Q My friend says tampons can get lost inside you – is that true?

No, it's physically impossible! Your cervix is in the way and the hole in it is far too tiny for a tampon to go through. The worst that can happen is that you can't find your tampon string – it's almost unknown for them to come off, but very occasionally the string gets tucked up inside your vagina. It's still not a problem – you'll probably be able to find it with your fingers. (It helps if you squat and push as if you were going to the loo.) In the unlikely event that you can't get it out, a nurse or doctor will certainly be able to.

COME OUT wherever you are!!!

Q I had my first period three months ago. The next month, nothing happened, but now I've come on again – what's happening?

Your hormones are just taking a while to settle down. Periods are often irregular for the first 2 years. Sometimes you have one, then nothing happens for several months. Worrying, feeling ill or just a change of routine (like going on holiday) can also make your periods late or early.

Q My periods are 32 days apart. Shouldn't they come every 28 days?

On average, women have a period every 28 days, but it can vary from 20 to 35.

Q Gran says I shouldn't wash my hair when I have my period – is she right?

In Gran's day, there were all sorts of myths about what you couldn't do when you had a period – for some weird reason, you weren't meant to eat ice cream! In reality, you can do everything you normally do – including swimming, having a bath and washing your hair.

No thanks... It's the wrong time of the month!

GET THIS!
6% of women use no protection at all during their period.

PRIMITIVE BELIEFS ABOUT PERIODS

✵ Shamans used to think menstrual blood was a source of supernatural power.

✵ The Ancient Babylonians thought that a menstruating woman would contaminate everything she touched – if she touched a sack of grain, it was destroyed.

✵ In Ancient Egypt, women had to take special cleansing baths when their periods finished – orthodox Jewish women still follow a similar ritual in a bath called a *mikveh*.

✵ In the Chinese province of Tsinghai, a girl mustn't allow her menstrual blood to touch the earth in case it offends the Earth Spirit. To stop this happening, she is supposed to fasten her trousers to her ankles. (Try doing that in flares!)

✵ In medieval times, it was a sin for a woman to go to church if she was having a period.

✵ In Mediterranean societies, it is traditional to slap a girl's face when she starts her first period, one reason being to bring colour back into her pale cheeks. Ouch!

Worst Case Scenario

My friend had her first period during PE. EVERYONE saw the blood on her shorts. I'm scared it might happen to me. How can I avoid it?

It can be hard to tell when your first period is due. Some girls get a crampy feeling in their abdomen or lower back, others notice a brownish stain in their pants or spots of watery blood. Some feel weepy or tetchy, but others have no symptoms at all – but don't be scared, be prepared! Here's how:

✿ Wear a panty liner on PE days and public occasions. Period blood doesn't gush out – it trickles through gradually over a few days. A panty liner should spare your blushes until you can get hold of a sanitary towel and freshen up.

✿ Carry change for the sanitary towel machine, a change of pants, a small pack of travel wipes and a press-on sanitary towel in a plastic bag or make-up bag.

✿ If your period starts unexpectedly, go to the nearest loo. Put the grotty knickers in the bag, then freshen up with wipes. Put the press-on towel in the spare knickers and put them on. If you haven't got a towel, a pad of folded tissues or soft loo roll tucked in your pants will work in an emergency.

✿ If you get a little bit of blood on your skirt, try dabbing it out with a paper towel soaked in cold water (hot water will set the stain). Dry under the hand-dryer.

✿ If the stain is really obvious and you're at school, you have three options:
a) Tie your sweatshirt round your waist to cover it up.
b) Ask your mate to blag a change of clothes from Lost Property.
c) Find your favourite teacher and ask for help. (She's trained to deal with these things discreetly.)

Q My friend says it's impossible to get pregnant if you have sex during your period — is she right?

This is all your fault! You got me **pregnant!**

No! You CAN get pregnant if you have sex during your period. Some girls (maybe you, maybe her) ovulate 2 or 3 days after their periods start, which means there could well be a nice, ripe egg waiting in the wings to be fertilized by the first sperm that pops in to say hello. It's impossible to tell when you're ovulating because your body sometimes pulls a fast one and your cycle changes without warning. The only sure-fire way to avoid pregnancy is not to have sex. Your second best bet is to use a reliable method of contraception every single time – without fail. Run and tell your mate before it's too late!

Q Help! My period pains make me want to go to bed and curl up in a ball.

Now you know why Grandma used to call it "The Curse". Some girls sail through their periods without a twinge but around 80% of us get various aches and pains – it's a hormone thing. The discomfort you can feel is your uterus contracting, due to an excess of prostaglandins. This can cause spasms, abdominal cramp, aching backs and thighs – hardly a barrel of laughs, but rarely anything to worry about. If you feel dizzy, sick, have diarrhoea or a pain that won't go, see a doctor. Otherwise, try these tips...

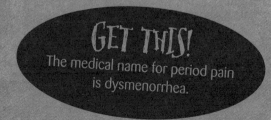

GET THIS!
The medical name for period pain is dysmenorrhea.

HOW TO MAKE PERIODS LESS OF A PAIN

✳ Ask your mum for some paracetamol or painkillers containing Ibuprofen.

✳ Gently rub your abdomen.

✳ Do some gentle exercises and stretches. This will release endorphins, your body's natural "painkillers", and reduce that bloated, puffy feeling.

✳ Cut out junk food and eat plenty of fruit and veg. A week before, avoid salt, white flour, and caffeine (found in fizzy drinks, tea, coffee and chocolate).

✳ Try herbal teas – mint tea helps to ease cramp; raspberry leaf tea helps to relieve bloating and pains.

✳ Have a warm bath and curl up with a hot-water bottle – heat eases cramp.

1 Sit on the floor with your legs wide apart. Hold your toes or clasp your ankles. Keep your back straight and breathe in, holding your diaphragm (the muscles under your ribs) up and in. Take a few breaths. As you breathe out for the last time, bend forwards towards the floor.

----

2 Sit with your knees open and bent to the sides, with the soles of your feet pressed together. Clasp your hands under your toes or hold your ankles. Breathe in deeply, expanding your chest and lifting your diaphragm. Raise your head and feel your stomach expand. Breathe deeply 5 times.

----

3 Lie on your back with one leg stretched out and pull the other knee up to your chin. Clasp your knee with your arms to ease the strain and hold the posture, relaxing for a few minutes.

----

4 Stand with your feet apart and move your hips in a full circle – twice in one direction, then twice in the other. Repeat 10 times.

Q Will I have periods for ever and ever?

No. From about the age of 40, you start running out of decent eggs. They don't always mature properly and you don't ovulate as often. The level of your female hormones starts to drop, your periods become fewer, then one day they stop altogether, often when you are around 50. The time when they stop is called the menopause, otherwise known as the change of life. Once you've had the change, you can't get pregnant.

GET THIS!

Woman are the only animals unable to have babies for the whole of their lifetime. In all other species, female animals remain fertile until they die.

Q A few days each month, I turn into the bitch from hell! I'm not usually like this – am I going mad?

Oh no, it sounds like the dreaded PMT (premenstrual tension). It's not an illness as such – it's a truck-load of physical and emotional symptoms that some of us get in the days leading up to our periods. Some girls just feel a bit weepy and tired, others feel horrible, hateful and flip their lids over the slightest thing. No one knows what really causes it, but most experts reckon hormones are to blame.

YOU ATE THE LAST BISCUIT!

PMT SYMPTOMS

1 A few days each month, your waistbands are too tight and your bras are too small.
REASON WHY: Either you put them in the boil wash or it's premenstrual fluid retention.

2 Normally he's a babe, but today your boyfriend is so irritating you want to hit him in the nuts with a tea tray.
REASON WHY: Either he really is irritating or you're suffering from premenstrual mood swings.

3 For no good reason, you want to jump off a cliff.
REASON WHY: Either you're into hang-gliding or you have premenstrual blues.

4 Suddenly, you look like a pig in lycra.
REASON WHY: Either you're wearing your kid sister's skirt or you have premenstrual weight gain.

5 You seem to be growing a horn on your nose.
REASON WHY: Either you're a unicorn or you're getting a premenstrual zit.

6 You have just eaten 3 tubes of Pringles, a big, fat cake and a box of chocolate fingers.
REASON WHY: Either you're a hippo and it's your birthday or you have premenstrual carbohydrate cravings.

7 You feel like you've been hit over the head with a tea tray.
REASON WHY: Either your boyfriend is defending himself against you or you have a premenstrual headache.

8 The slightest thing makes you b–b–burst into

wahhhhhhhhh!

REASON WHY: Either you've been watching *Bambi* or you have pre-menstrual weepies.

Q My auntie said she couldn't go swimming because it was the wrong time of the month. What did she mean?

"Wrong time of the month" is another way of saying you're having a period. In the past, it wasn't done to talk about periods, so code words were used instead. Today, most women are much more laid-back about menstruation, but just for fun, here are some expressions you might come across...

✿ Up on blocks.

✿ It's Rag Week.

✿ I've got the painters in.

✿ Red sails in the sunset.

✿ I've got my monthlies.

✿ I've got the Curse.

✿ It's the wrong time of the month.

✿ Arsenal are at home.

✿ Chasing the cotton mouse.

✿ I've got the flags out.

✿ I'm surfing the crimson wave.

SO NOW YOU KNOW...

Now that you know all about big girls'
bumpy parts, foldy flaps and furry bits
there may be a burning question you're still
dying to ask about puberty:

WHY ME?!

OK, it's not just you.
It's every girl who ever walked the planet.
There will be good days and bad days, but
you mustn't take puberty personally. It's
just a sticky in-between stage that happens
to everyone. Even the Queen.

It helps to talk about what you're going
through. Talk to your friends, your mum or
dad, your sisters and grandma. If you can't
talk to them and you're worried, speak to
an expert. And on sad, mad, paper bag
days, remember this: puberty won't last for
ever – it's physically impossible!

So ... hang on in there. Go with the flow
(period joke – keep your sense of humour!).
'Cos when it's all over, you'll feel like a
new woman!

INDEX

Where Next? For further advice, check out:
Being Girl: www.beinggirl.co.uk
BBC Teens: www.bbc.co.uk/teens
ChildLine: 0800 11 11 • www.childline.co.uk
Tampax: www.tampax.co.uk